The Best of Robert Service

Robert W. Service

Illustrations by Mariken van Nimwegen

hancock
house

ISBN 0-88839-545-0
Copyright © 2004 Hancock House

Cataloging in Publication Data

Service, Robert W., 1874-1958
    The best of Robert Service / by Robert Service ; illustrations
by Mariken Van Nimwegen.

Poems.
ISBN 0-88839-545-0

    I. Van Nimwegen, Mariken II. Title.

PS8537.E78A17 2004   C811'.52   C2003-906514-6

Printed in Indonesia—TK Printing

Published simultaneously in Canada and the United States by

HANCOCK HOUSE PUBLISHERS LTD.
19313 Zero Avenue, Surrey, B.C. V3S 9R9
(604) 538-1114 Fax (604) 538-2262

HANCOCK HOUSE PUBLISHERS
1431 Harrison Avenue, Blaine, WA 98230-5005
(604) 538-1114 Fax (604) 538-2262
Web Site: www.hancockhouse.com *Email:* sales@hancockhouse.com

Contents

Robert Service, 1911.

Robert Service

by Harriett Shlossberg

ROBERT SERVICE was born in Lancashire, England in 1874, the son of lower middle class parents, the eldest of what would be ten children. When he was four, the family moved to Glasgow, Scotland and he and a brother were taken to live with his paternal grandparents and four aunts nearby in Kilwinning. In school, he was known for getting into scrapes, but mostly was a solitary and imaginative child, immersing himself in books. At a celebratory meal for his sixth birthday, he always remembered surprising the adults and even himself, with two spontaneous rhyming verses in the form of a grace, foretelling of his future and his talents.

When his parents came to visit him at last, his mother was so shocked to discover him wearing a kilt and nothing beneath it, she took him home to Glasgow and his family. Bored by school, he submerged himself in books to his liking, reading Shakespeare, Burns, Longfellow, tales of adventure, and declamatory verses. At fourteen, it was suggested he leave school, and soon he was apprenticed as a clerk in a bank. There, with time on his hands, he began rhyming and making verses and by age sixteen, had over a dozen poems published in local newspapers. Throughout his late teens and early twenties, he dreamed of travelling and adventure, of escaping the bank. Finally, at twenty-two, he resigned, and in 1896, headed for Canada.

For the next eight years Robert was mostly a wanderer up and down the West Coast of Canada and the U.S., lingering sometimes, trying his hand at ranching and farming, even manual labor and running a store, often living on as little as twenty-five cents a day in rough conditions.

All the time he was observing landscape and characters of every description. Desperate for an easier way of living, in Victoria in 1903, he took a job with the Canadian Bank of Commerce, and after a brief stint there was transferred to Kamloops, and then to Whitehorse in the Yukon Territory. He was fascinated with the history of this area, the characters drawn to it, the tales of the gold rush, and the natural beauty in which he tramped alone for endless hours. It was here that he was asked to prepare an original reading for an entertainment. When he was almost shot in the head by a zealous bank clerk who thought he was a burglar, the inspiration for "The Shooting of Dan McGrew" was born. A month later, while at a party, he heard a story that gave him the idea for "The Cremation of Sam McGee". These, along with other poems that came pouring out at this time, were published in 1907 in a book he called *Songs of a Sourdough*, a reference to the bread starter carried by the miners. In 1908, the bank sent him to Dawson, and there he put his energies into a second volume of verse. He soon realized that he could make enough money from his writing to obtain freedom from the necessity of formal work and could indulge in the dreaming, loafing and outdoor roaming he loved to do. Gradually, these books became widely known, and the royalties started flowing in, which would be the case for the rest of his long life. The next year, he resigned from the bank, rented a cabin and worked on a novel called *The Trail of Ninety-Eight*, about the gold rush to the Klondike, which was published in 1910. He then undertook to make the 2,000 mile journey from Edmonton to the Klondike himself, re-creating the trek the prospectors made, which gave rise to more poems rooted in the northern experience, and a book called *Rhymes of a Rolling Stone*. By this time war was breaking out in the Balkans, and he was asked by the Toronto Star to be a correspondent for them, which, in his never ending quest for adventure, he accepted.

That was the end of his time in the Yukon, and the start of long travels in Europe. After the First World War, in which he volunteered as an ambulance driver, he lived most of his life in France. Robert Service, recognized as the most read balladeer of the twentieth century, continued to write and be published into his mid-eighties. He said, "I just go for a walk and come back with a poem in my pocket." He died at his home in Lancieux, in Brittany, in 1958.

During the summer months recitals of his ballads at his cabins in Dawson City and Whitehorse draw great crowds. And many of the American and Canadian towns in which he worked, Duncan, Seattle, Portland, San Francisco and Los Angeles hold festivals or readings to celebrate this man who captured so much of the color of an earlier era.

Opposite page: *Robert Service at his cabin, Dawson, 1910.*

Right: *Robert Service in his cabin, Dawson, 1911.*

The Spell of the Yukon

I wanted the gold, and I got it;
I scrabbled and mucked like a slave.
Was it famine or scurvy, I fought it;
I hurled my youth into a grave.
I wanted the gold and I got it—
Came out with a fortune last fall,—
Yet somehow life's not what I thought it,
And somehow the gold isn't all.

No! There's the land. (Have you seen it?)
It's the cussedest land that I know,
From the big, dizzy mountains that screen it
To the deep, deathlike valleys below.
Some say God was tired when He made it;
Some say it's a fine land to shun;
Maybe; but there's some as would trade it
For no land on earth—and I'm one.
You come to get rich (damned good reason);
You feel like an exile at first.
You hate it like hell for a season,
And then you are worse than the worst.
It grips you like some kinds of sinning;
It twists you from foe to a friend;
It seems it's been since the beginning;
It seems it will be to the end.

I've stood on some mighty-mouthed hollow
That's plumb-full of hush to the brim.
I've watched the big, husky sun wallow
In crimson and gold, and grow dim,
Till the moon set the pearly peaks gleaming,
And the stars tumbled out, neck and crop;
And I've thought that I surely was dreaming,
With the peace o' the world piled on top.

The summer—no sweeter was ever;
The sunshiny woods all athrill;
The grayling aleap in the river,
The bighorn asleep on the hill.
The strong life that never knows harness;
The wilds where the caribou call;
The Freshness, the freedom, the farness—
O God, how I'm stuck on it all!

The winter! the brightness that blinds you,
The white land locked tight as a drum,
The cold fear that follows and finds you,
The silence that bludgeons you dumb.
The snows that are older than history,
The woods where the weird shadows slant;
The stillness, the moonlight, the mystery,
I've bade 'em good-bye—but I can't.

There's a land where the mountains are nameless,
  And the rivers all run God knows where;
There are lives that are erring and aimless,
  And deaths that just hang by a hair.
There are hardships that nobody reckons;
  There are valleys unpeopled and still;
There's a land—oh, it beckons and beckons,
  And I want to go back—and I will.

◆

They're making my money diminish;
  I'm sick of the taste of champagne.
Thank God! when I'm skinned to a finish
  I'll pike to the Yukon again.

I'll fight—and you bet it's no sham-fight;
It's hell! but I've been there before;
And it's better than this by a damn sight—
So me for the Yukon once more.

There's gold, and it's haunting and haunting;
It's luring me on as of old;
Yet it isn't the gold that I'm wanting
So much as just finding the gold.
It's the great, big, broad land 'way up yonder,
It's the forests where silence has lease,
It's the beauty that fills me with wonder,
It's the stillness that fills me with peace.

My Friends

The man above was a murderer,
the man below was a thief;
And I lay there in the bunk between,
ailing beyond belief;
A weary armful of skin and bone,
wasted with pain and grief.

My feet were froze, and the lifeless toes
were purple and green and gray.
The little flesh that clung to my bones,
you could punch in it holes like clay;
The skin on my gums was a sullen black,
and slowly peeling away.

I was sure enough in a direful fix,
and often I wondered why
They did not take the chance that was left
and leave me alone to die,
Or finish me off with a dose of dope—
So utterly lost was I.

But no; they brewed me the green-spruce tea,
and nursed me there like a child;
And the homicide, he was good to me,
and bathed my sores and smiled;

And the thief, he starved that I might be fed,
and his eyes were kind and mild.

◆

Yet they were woefully wicked men,
and often at night in pain
I heard the murderer speak of his deed
and dream it over again;
I heard the poor thief sorrowing for
the dead self he had slain.

◆

I'll never forget that bitter dawn,
so evil, askew and gray,
When they wrapped me round in the skins of beasts
and they bore me to a sleigh,
And we started out with the nearest post
an hundred miles away.

◆

I'll never forget the trail they broke,
with its tense, unuttered woe;
And the crunch, crunch, crunch as their snowshoes sank
through the crust of the hollow snow;
And my breath would fail, and every beat
of my heart was like a blow.

◆

And oftentimes I would die the death,
yet wake me up anew;
The sun would be all ablaze on the waste,
and the sky a blighting blue,
And the tears would rise in my snow-blind eyes
and furrow my cheeks like dew.

◆

And the camps we made when their strength outplayed
and the day was pinched and wan;
And oh, the joy of that blessed halt,
and how I did dread the dawn;
And how I hated the weary men
who rose and dragged me on.

◆

And oh, how I begged to rest, to rest—
the snow was so sweet a shroud!
And oh, how I cried when they urged me on,
cried and cursed them aloud!
Yet on they strained, all racked and pained,
and sorely their backs were bowed.

◆

And then it was all like a lurid dream,
and I prayed for a swift release
From the ruthless ones who would not leave
me to die alone in peace;
Till I wakened up and I found myself
at the post of the Mounted Police.

◆

And there was my friend the murderer,
and there was my friend the thief,
With bracelets of steel around their wrists,
and wicked beyond belief:
But when they come to God's judgement seat—
may I be allowed the brief.

The Cremation of Sam McGee

There are strange things done in the midnight sun
By the men who moil for gold;
The Arctic trails have their secret tales
That would make your blood run cold;
The Northern Lights have seen queer sights,
But the queerest they ever did see
Was that night on the marge of Lake Lebarge
I cremated Sam McGee.

Now Sam McGee was from Tennessee,
where the cotton blooms and blows.
Why he left his home in the South to roam
'round the Pole, God only knows.
He was always cold, but the land of gold
seemed to hold him like a spell;
Though he'd often say in his homely way
that he'd "sooner live in Hell."

On a Christmas Day we were mushing our way
over the Dawson trail.
Talk of your cold! through the parka's fold
it stabbed like a driven nail.
If our eyes we'd close, then the lashes froze
till sometimes we couldn't see,
It wasn't much fun, but the only one
to whimper was Sam McGee.

And that very night, as we lay packed tight
in our robes beneath the snow,
And the dogs were fed, and the stars o'erhead
were dancing heel and toe,
He turned to me, and "Cap," says he,
"I'll cash in this trip, I guess;
And if I do, I'm asking that you
won't refuse my last request."

◆

Well, he seemed so low that I couldn't say no;
then he says with a sort of moan,
"It's the cursed cold, and it's got right hold
till I'm chilled clean through to the bone.
Yet 'taint being dead—it's my awful dread
of the icy grave that pains.
So I want you to swear that, foul or fair,
you'll cremate my last remains."

◆

A pal's last need is a thing to heed,
so I swore I would not fail;
And we started on at the streak of dawn;
but God! he looked ghastly pale.
He crouched on the sleigh, and he raved all day
of his home in Tennessee;
And before nightfall a corpse was all
that was left of Sam McGee.
There wasn't a breath in that land of death,
and I hurried, horror-driven,

With a corpse half hid that I couldn't get rid,
because of a promise given;
It was lashed to the sleigh, and it seemed to say:
"You may tax your brawn and brains,
But you promised true, and it's up to you
to cremate these last remains."

◆

Now a promise made is a debt unpaid,
and the trail has its own stern code.
In the days to come, though my lips were dumb,
in my heart how I cursed that load!
In the long, long night, by the lone firelight,
while the huskies, round in a ring,
Howled out their woes to the homeless snows—
Oh God, how I loathed the thing!

◆

And every day that quiet clay
seemed to heavy and heavier grow;
And on I went, though the dogs were spent
and the grub was getting low.
The trail was bad, and I felt half mad,
but I swore I would not give in;
And I'd often sing to the hateful thing,
and it hearkened with a grin.

◆

Till I came to the marge of Lake Lebarge,
and a derelict there lay;

It was jammed in the ice, but I saw in a trice
it was called the *Alice May*.
And I looked at it, and I thought a bit,
and I looked at my frozen chum;
Then "Here," said I, with a sudden cry,
"is my cre-ma-tor-eum!"

◆

Some planks I tore from the cabin floor,
and I lit the boiler fire;
Some coal I found that was lying around,
and I heaped the fuel higher;
The flames just soared, and the furnace roared—
such a blaze you seldom see,
And I burrowed a hole in the glowing coal,
and I stuffed in Sam McGee.

◆

Then I made a hike, for I didn't like
to hear him sizzle so;
And the heavens scowled, and the huskies howled,
and the wind began to blow.
It was icy cold, but the hot sweat rolled
down my cheeks, and I don't know why;
And the greasy smoke in an inky cloak
went streaking down the sky.

◆

I do not know how long in the snow
I wrestled with grisly fear;

23

But the stars came out and they danced about
ere again I ventured near;
I was sick with dread, but I bravely said,
"I'll just take a peep inside.
I guess he's cooked, and it's time I looked."
Then the door I opened wide.

◆

And there sat Sam, looking cool and calm,
in the heart of the furnace roar;
And he wore a smile you could see a mile,
and he said, "Please close that door.
It's fine in here, but I greatly fear
you'll let in the cold and storm—
Since I left Plumtree, down in Tennessee,
it's the first time I've been warm."

◆

There are strange things done in the midnight sun
By the men who moil for gold;
The Arctic trails have their secret tales
That would make your blood run cold;
The Northern Lights have seen queer sights,
But the queerest they ever did see
Was that night on the marge of Lake Lebarge
I cremated Sam McGee.

The Telegraph Operator

I will not wash my face;
I will not brush my hair;
I "pig" around the place—
There's nobody to care.
Nothing but rock and tree;
Nothing but wood and stone,
Oh, God, it's hell to be
Alone, alone, alone!

◆

Snow-peaks and deep-gashed draws
Corral me in a ring.
I feel as if I was
The only living thing
On all this blighted earth;
And so I frowst and shrink,
And crouching by my hearth
I hear the thoughts I think.

◆

I think of all I miss—
The boys I used to know;
The girls I used to kiss;
The coin I used to blow;
The bars I used to haunt;
The racket and the row;
The beers I didn't want
(I wish I had 'em now).
Day after day the same,

Only a little worse;
No one to grouch or blame—
Oh, for a loving curse!
Oh, in the night I fear,
Haunted by nameless things,
Just for a voice to cheer,
Just for a hand that clings!

Faintly as from a star
Voices come o'er the line;
Voices of ghosts afar,
Not in this world of mine
Lives in whose loom I grope;
Words in whose weft I hear
Eager the thrill of hope,
Awful the chill of fear.

I'm thinking out aloud;
I reckon that is bad;
(The snow is like a shroud)—
Maybe I'm going mad.

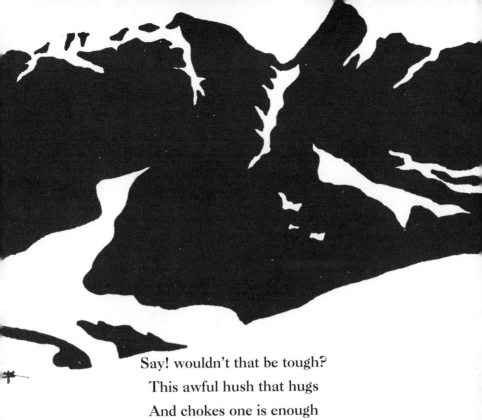

Say! wouldn't that be tough?
This awful hush that hugs
And chokes one is enough
To make a man go "bugs."

There's not a thing to do;
I cannot sleep at night;
No wonder I'm so blue;
Oh, for a friendly fight!
The din and rush of strife;
A music-hall aglow;
A crowd, a city, life—
Dear God, I miss it so!

Here, you have moped enough!
Brace up and play the game!
But say, it's awful tough—

Day after day the same
(I've said that twice, I bet).
Well, there's not much to say.
I wish I had a pet,
Or something I could play.

Cheer up! don't get so glum
And sick of everything.
The worst is yet to come;
God help you till the Spring.
God shield you from the Fear;
Teach you to laugh, not moan.
Ha! ha! it sounds so queer—
Alone, alone, alone!

Clancy of the Mounted Police

In the little Crimson Manual
it's written plain and clear
That who would wear the scarlet coat
shall say good-bye to fear;
Shall be a guardian of the right,
a sleuth-hound of the trail—
In the little Crimson Manual
there's no such word as "fail"—
Shall follow on, though heavens fall,
or Hell's top-turrets freeze,
Half round the world, if need there be,
on bleeding hands and knees.

◆

It's duty, duty, first and last,
the Crimson Manual saith;
The Scarlet Riders make reply:
"It's duty—to the death."
And so they sweep the solitudes,
free men from all the earth;
And so they sentinel the woods,
the wilds that know their worth;
And so they scour the startled plains
and mock at hurt and pain,
And read their Crimson Manual,
and find their duty plain.

Knights of the lists of unrenown,
born of the frontier's need,
Disdainful of the spoken word,
exultant in the deed;
Unconscious heroes of the waste,
proud players of the game,
Props of the power behind the throne,
upholders of the name;
For thus the Great White Chief hath said:
"In all my lands be peace,"
And so to maintain his word he gave
his West the Scarlet Police.

◆

Livid-lipped was the valley,
still as the grave of God;
Misty shadows of mountain
thinned into mists of cloud;
Corpselike and stark was the land,
with a quiet that crushed and awed,
And the stars of the weird sub-arctic
glimmered over its shroud.

Deep in the trench of the valley
two men stationed the Post,
Seymour and Clancy the reckless,
fresh from the long patrol;
Seymour, the sergeant, and Clancy—
Clancy who made his boast
He could cinch like a bronco the Northland,
and cling to the prongs of the Pole.

◆

Two lone men on detachment,
standing for law on the trail;
Undismayed in the vastness,
wise with the wisdom of old—
Out of the night hailed a half-breed
telling a pitiful tale:
"White man starving and crazy
on the banks of the Nordenscold."

◆

Up sprang the red-haired Clancy,
lean and eager of eye;
Loaded the long toboggan,
strapped each dog at its post;
Whirled his lash at the leader;
then, with a whoop and a cry,
Into the Great White Silence
faded away like a ghost.
The clouds were a misty shadow,
the hills were a shadowy mist;

Sunless, voiceless and pulseless,
the day was a dream of woe;
Through the ice-rifts the river
smoked and bubbled and hissed;
Behind was a trail fresh broken,
in front the untrodden snow.

Ahead of the dogs ploughed Clancy,
haloed by steaming breath;
Through peril of open water,
through ache of insensate cold;
Up rivers wantonly winding
in a land affianced to death,
Till he came to a cowering cabin
on the banks of the Nordenscold.

Then Clancy loosed his revolver,
and he strode through the open door;
And there was the man he sought for,
crouching beside the fire;
The hair of his beard was singeing,
the frost on his back was hoar,
And ever he crooned and chanted
as if he never would tire:—

"I panned and I panned in the shiny sand,
and I sniped on the river bar;
But I know, I know, that it's down below

that the golden treasures are;
So I'll wait and wait till the floods abate,
and I'll sink a shaft once more,
And I'd like to bet that I'll go home yet
with a brass-band playing before."

◆

He was nigh as thin as a sliver,
and he whined like a Moose-hide cur;
So Clancy clothed him and nursed him
as a mother nurses a child;
Lifted him on the toboggan,
wrapped him in robes of fur,
Then with the dogs sore straining
started to face the Wild.

◆

Said the Wild, "I will crush this Clancy,
so fearless and insolent;
For him will I loose my fury,
and blind and buffet and beat;
Pile up my snows to stay him;
then when his strength is spent,
Leap on him from my ambush
and crush him under my feet.

◆

"Him will I ring with my silence,
compass him with my cold;
Closer and closer clutch him
unto mine icy breast;

Buffet him with my blizzards,
deep in my snows enfold,
Claiming his life as my tribute,
giving my wolves the rest."

Clancy crawled through the vastness;
o'er him the hate of the Wild;
Full on his face fell the blizzard;
cheering his huskies he ran;
Fighting, fierce-heated and tireless,
snows that drifted and piled,
With ever and ever behind him
singing the crazy man:

"Sing hey, sing ho, for the ice and snow,
And a heart that's ever merry;
Let us trim and square with a lover's care
—For why should a man be sorry?—
A grave deep, deep with the moon a-peep,
A grave in the frozen mold.
Sing hey, sing ho, for the winds that blow,
And a grave deep down in the ice and snow,
A grave in the land of gold."
Day after day of darkness,
the whirl of the seething snows;
Day after day of blindness,
the swoop of the stinging blast;
On through a blur of fury

the swing of staggering blows;
On through a world of turmoil,
empty, inane and vast.

Night with its writhing storm-whirl,
night despairingly black;
Night with its hours of terror,
numb and endlessly long;
Night with its weary waiting,
fighting the shadows back,
And ever the crouching madman
singing his crazy song.

Cold with its creeping terror,
cold with its sudden clinch;
Cold so utter you wonder
if 'twill ever again be warm;
Clancy grinned as he shuddered,
"Surely it isn't a cinch
Being wet-nurse to a looney
in the teeth of an arctic storm."

The blizzard passed and the dawn broke,
knife-edged and crystal clear;
The sky was a blue-domed iceberg,
sunshine outlawed away;
Ever by snowslide and ice-rip
haunted and hovered the Fear;

Ever the Wild malignant
poised and panted to slay.

◆

The lead-dog freezes in harness—
cut him out of the team!
The lung of the wheel-dog's bleeding—
shoot him and let him lie!
On and on with the others—
lash them until they scream!
"Pull for your lives, you devils!
On! To halt is to die."

◆

There in the frozen vastness
Clancy fought with his foes;
The ache of the stiffened fingers,
the cut of the showshoe thong;
Cheeks black-raw through the hood-flap,
eyes that tingled and closed,
And ever to urge and cheer him
quavered the madman's song.
Colder it grew and colder,
till the last heat left the earth,
And there in the great stark stillness
the bale fires glinted and gleamed,
And the Wild all around exulted

and shook with a devilish mirth,
And life was far and forgotten,
the ghost of a joy once dreamed.

◆

Death! And one who defied it,
a man of the Mounted Police;
Fought it there to a standstill
long after hope was gone;
Grinned through his bitter anguish,
fought without let or cease,
Suffering, straining, striving,
stumbling, struggling on,

Till the dogs lay down in their traces,
and rose and staggered and fell;
Till the eys of him dimmed with shadows,
and the trail was so hard to see;
Till the Wild howled out triumphant,
and the world was a frozen hell—
Then said Constable Clancy:
"I guess that it's up to me."

◆

Far down the trail they saw him,
and his hands, they were blanched like bone;
His face was a blackened horror,

from his eye-lids the salt rheum ran.
His feet he was lifting strangely,
    as if they were made of stone,
But safe in his arms and sleeping
    he carried the crazy man.

So Clancy got into Barracks,
    and the boys made rather a scene;
And the O.C. called him a hero,
    and was nice as a man could be;
But Clancy gazed down his trousers
    at the place where his toes had been,
And then he howled like a husky,
    and sang in a shaky key;

"When I go back to the old love
    that's true to the finger-tips,
I'll say: 'Here's bushels of gold, love,'
    and I'll kiss my girl on the lips;
'It's yours to have and to hold, love.'
    It's the proud, proud boy I'll be,
When I go back to the old love
    That's waited so long for me."

The Ballad of Hard Luck Henry

Now wouldn't you expect to find
a man an awful crank
That's staked out night three hundred claims,
and every one a blank;
That's followed every fool stampede,
and seen the rise and fall
Of camps where men got gold in chunks
and he got none at all;
That's prospected a bit of ground
and sold it for a song
To see it yield a fortune to
some fool that came along;
That's sunk a dozen bedrock holes,
and not a speck in sight,
Yet sees them take a million
from the claims to left and right?
Now aren't things like that enough
to drive a man to booze?
But Hard-Luck Smith was hoodoo-proof—
he knew the way to lose.

◆

'Twas in the fall of nineteen-four—
leap-year I've heard them say—
When Hard-Luck came to Hunker Creek
and took a hillside lay.
And lo! as if to make amends

for all the futile past,
Late in the year he struck it rich,
the real pay-streak at last.
The riffles of his sluicing-box
were choked with speckled earth,
And night and day he worked that lay
for all that he was worth.
And when in chill December's gloom
his lucky lease expired,
He found that he had made a stake
as big as he desired.

One day while meditating on
the waywardness of fate,
He felt the ache of a lonely man
to find a fitting mate;
A petticoated pard to cheer
his solitary life,
A woman with soft, soothing ways,
a confidante, a wife.
And while he cooked his supper
on his little Yukon stove,
He wished that he had staked a claim
in Love's rich treasure-trove;
When suddenly he paused and held
aloft a Yukon egg,
For there in pencilled letters
was the magic name of Peg.
You know these Yukon eggs of ours—

some pink, some green, some blue—
A dollar per, assorted tints, assorted flavors, too!
The supercilious cheechako
might designate them high,
But one acquires a taste for them
and likes them by-and-by.
Well, Hard-Luck Henry took this egg
and held it to the light,
And there was more faint pencilling
that sorely taxed his sight.
At last he made it out, and then
the legend ran like this—
"Will Klondike miner write to Peg,
Plumhollow, Squashville, Wis.?"

◆

That night he got to thinking of
this far-off, unknown fair;
It seemed so sort of opportune,
an answer to his prayer.

She flitted sweetly through his dreams,
she haunted him by day,
She smiled through clouds of nicotine,
she cheered his weary way.
At last he yielded to the spell;
his course of love he set—
Wisconsin his objective point,
his object, Margaret.
With every mile of sea and land

his longing grew and grew.
He practiced all his pretty words,
and these, I fear, were few.
At last, one frosty evening,
with a cold chill down his spine,
He found himself before her house,
the threshold of the shrine.
His courage flickered to a spark,
then glowed with sudden flame.
He knocked; he heard a welcome word;
she came—his goddess came!
Oh, she was fair as any flower,
and huskily he spoke:
"I'm all the way from Klondike, with
a mighty heavy poke.
I'm looking for a lassie, one
whose Christian name is Peg,
Who sought a Klondike miner,
and who wrote it on an egg."

◆

47

The lassie gazed at him a space,
her cheeks grew rosy red.
She gazed at him with tear-bright eyes,
then tenderly she said:
"Yes, lonely Klondike miner,
it is true my name is Peg.
It's also true I longed for you
and wrote it on an egg.

48

My heart went out to someone in
    that land of night and cold;
But oh, I fear that Yukon egg
    must have been mighty old.
I waited long, I hoped and feared;
    you should have come before;
I've been a wedded woman now
    for eighteen months or more.
I'm sorry, since you've come so far,
    you ain't the one that wins;
But won't you take a step inside?
    I'll let you see the twins!"

Premonition

'Twas a year ago and the moon was bright
(Oh, I remember so well, so well);
I walked with my love in a sea of light,
And the voice of my sweet was a silver bell.
And sudden the moon grew strangely dull,
And sudden my love had taken wing;
I looked on the face of a grinning skull.
I strained to my heart a ghastly thing.

'Twas but fantasy, for my love lay still
In my arms, with her tender eyes aglow.
And she wondered why my lips were chill,
Why I was silent and kissed her so.
A year has gone and the moon is bright,
A gibbous moon, like a ghost of woe;
I sit by a new-made grave tonight,
And my heart is broken—it's strange, you know.

The Ballad of Blasphemous Bill

I took a contract to bury the body
of blasphemous Bill MacKie,
Whenever, wherever or whatsoever
the manner of death he die—
Whether he die in the light o' day
or under the peak-faced moon;
In cabin or dance-hall, camp or dive,
mucklucks or patent shoon;
On velvet tundra or virgin peak,
by glacier, drift or draw;
In muskeg hollow or canyon gloom,
by avalanche, fang or claw;
By battle, murder or sudden wealth,
by pestilence, "hooch" or lead—
I swore on the Book I would follow and look
till I found my tombless dead.

For Bill was a dainty kind of cuss,
and his mind was mighty sot
On a dinky patch with flowers and grass
in a civilized boneyard lot.
And where he died or how he died,
it didn't matter a damn
So long as he had a grave with frills
and a tombstone epigram.
So I promised him, and he paid the price
in good cheechako coin
(Which the same I blowed on that very night
down in the Tenderloin).
Then I painted a three-foot slab of pine:
"Here lies poor Bill MacKie,"
And I hung it up on my cabin wall
and I waited for Bill to die.

◆

Years passed away, and at last one day
came a squaw with a story strange,
· Of a long-deserted line of traps
'way back of the Bighorn range;
Of a little hut by the great divide,
and a white man stiff and still,
Lying there by his lonesome self,
and I figured it must be Bill.
So I thought of the contract I'd made with him,
and I took down from the shelf
The swell black box with the silver plate

he'd pcked out for hisself;
And I packed it full of grub and "hooch."
and I slung it on the sleigh;
Then I harnessed up my team of dogs
and was off at dawn of day.

You know what it's like in the Yukon wild
when it's sixty-nine below;
When the ice-worms wriggle their purple heads
through the crust of the pale blue snow;
When the pine trees crack like little guns
in the silence of the wood,
And the icicles hang down like tusks
under the parka hood;
When the stovepipe smoke breaks sudden off,
and the sky is weirdly lit,
And the careless feel of a bit of steel
burns like a red-hot spit;
When the mercury is a frozen ball,
and the frost-fiend stalks to kill—
Well, it was just like that that day
when I set out to look for Bill.

Oh, the awful hush that seemed to crush
me down on every hand,
As I blundered blind with a trail to find
through that blank and bitter land;
Half dazed, half crazed in the winter wild,

with its grim heart-breaking woes,
And the ruthless strife for a grip on life
that only the sourdough knows!
North by the compass, North I pressed;
river and peak and plain
Passed like a dream I slept to lose
and I waked to dream again.

◆

River and plain and mighty peak—
and who could stand unawed?
As their summits blazed, he could stand undazed
at the foot of the throne of God.
North, aye, North, through a land accurst,
shunned by the scouring brutes.
And all I heard was my own harsh word
and the whine of the malamutes,
Till at last I came to a cabin squat,
built in the side of a hill,
And I burst in the door, and there on the floor,
frozen to death, lay Bill.

◆

Ice, white ice, like a winding-sheet,
sheathing each smoke-grimed wall;
Ice on the stove-pipe, ice on the bed,
ice gleaming over all;
Sparkling ice on the dead man's chest,
glittering ice in his hair,
Ice on his fingers, ice in his heart,

ice in his glassy stare;
Hard as a log and trussed like a grog,
with his arms and legs outspread.
I gazed at the coffin I'd brought for him,
and I gazed at the gruesome dead,
And at last I spoke; "Bill liked his joke;
but still, goldarn his eyes,
A man had hought to consider his mates
in the way he goes and dies."

◆

Have you ever stood in an Arctic hut
in the shadow of the pole,
With a little coffin six by three
and a grief you can't control?
Have you ever sat by a frozen corpse
that looks at you with a grin,
And that seems to say: "You may try all day,
but you'll never jam me in?"
I'm not a man of the quitting kind,
but I never felt so blue
As I sat there gazing at that stiff
and studying what I'd do.
Then I rose and I kicked off the husky dogs
that were nosing round about,
And I lit a roaring fire in the stove,
and I started to thaw Bill out.

◆

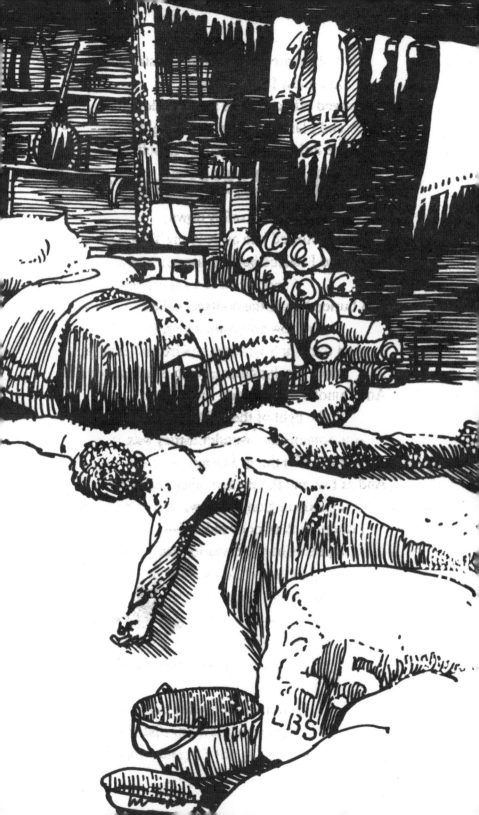

Well, I thawed and thawed for thirteen days,
but it didn't seem no good;
His arms and legs stuck out like pegs,
as if they was made of wood.
Till last I said: "It ain't no use—
he's froze too hard to thaw;
He's obstinate, and he won't lie straight,
so I guess I got to—saw."
So I sawed off poor Bill's arms and legs,
and I laid him snug and straight
In the little coffin he picked hisself,
with the dinky silver plate;
And I came nigh to near shedding a tear
as I nailed him safely down;
Then I stowed him away in my Yukon sleigh,
and I started back to town.

◆

So I buried him as the contract called
in a narrow grave and deep,
And there he's waiting the Great Clean-up,
when the Judgment sluice-heads sweep;
And I smoke my pipe and I meditate
in the light of the Midnight Sun,
And sometimes I wonder if they *was*,
the awful things I done.
And as I sit and the parson talks,
expounding on the Law,
I often think of poor old Bill—
and how hard he was to saw.

The Heart of the Sourdough

There, where the mighty mountains bare
their fangs unto the moon,
There, where the sullen sun-dogs glare
in the snow-bright, bitter noon,
And the glacier-gutted streams sweep down
at the clarion call of June.

◆

There, where the livid tundras keep
their tryst with the tranquil snows;
There, where the silences are spawned,
and the light of hell-fire flows
Into the bowl of the midnight sky, violet, amber and rose.

◆

There, where the rapids churn and roar,
and the ice-floes bellowing run;
Where the tortured, twisted rivers of blood
rush to the setting sun—
I've packed my kit and I'm going, boys,
ere another day is done.

◆

I knew it would call, or soon or late,
as it calls the whirring wings;
It's the olden lure, it's the golden lure,
it's the lure of the timeless things,
And tonight, oh, God of the trails untrod,
how it whines in my heart-strings!

I'm sick to death of your well-groomed gods,
    your make-believe and your show;
I long for a whiff of bacon and beans,
    a snug shakedown in the snow;
A trail to break, and a life at stake,
    and another bout with the foe.

♦

With the raw-ribbed Wild that abhors all life,
    the Wild that would crush and rend,
I have clinched and closed with the naked North,
    I have learned to defy and defend;
Shoulder to shoulder we have fought it out—
    yet the Wild must win in the end.

♦

I have flouted the Wild. I have followed its lure,
    fearless, familiar, alone;
By all that the battle means and makes
    I claim that land for my own;
Yet the Wild must win, and a day will come
    when I shall be overthrown.

♦

Then when, as wolf-dogs fight, we've fought,
    the lean wolf-land and I;
Fought and bled till the snows are red
    under the reeling sky;
Even as lean wolf-dogs go down
    will I go down and die.

The Three Voices

The waves have a story to tell me,
As I lie on the lonely beach;
Chanting aloft in the pine-tops,
The wind has a lesson to teach;
But the stars sing an anthem of glory
I cannot put into speech.

The waves tell of ocean spaces,
Of hearts that are wild and brave,
Of populous city places,
Of desolate shores they lave,
Of men who sally in quest of gold
To sink in an ocean grave.

The wind is a mighty roamer;
He bids me to keep free,
Clean from the taint of the gold-lust,
Hardy and pure as he;
Cling with my love to nature
As a child to the mother knee.

But the stars throng out in their glory,
And they sing of the God in man;
They sing of the Mighty Master,
Of the loom His fingers span.
Where a star or a soul is a part of the whole,
And weft in the wondrous plan.

Here by the camp-fire's flicker,
Deep in my blanket curled,
I long for the peace of the pine-gloom,
When the scroll of the Lord is unfurled,
And the wind and the wave are silent,
And world is singing to world.

64

The Men that Don't Fit In

There's a race of men that don't fit in,
A race that can't stay still;
So they break the hearts of kith and kin,
And they roam the world at will.
They range the field and they rove the flood,
And they climb the mountain's crest.
Theirs is the curse of the gypsy blood,
And they don't know how to rest.

◆

If they just went straight, they might go far;
They are strong and brave and true;
But they're always tired of the things that are,
And they want the strange and new.
They say: "Could I find my proper groove,
What a deep mark I would make!"
So they chop and change, and each fresh move
Is only a fresh mistake.

◆

And each forgets, as he strips and runs
With a brilliant, fitful pace,
It's the steady quiet, plodding ones
Who win in the lifelong race.
And each forgets that his youth has fled,
Forgets that his prime is past,
Till he stands one day with a hope that's dead,
In the glare of the truth at last.

◆

He has failed, he has failed;
   he has missed his chance;
He has just done things by half.
Life's been a jolly good joke on him,
   And now is the time to laugh.
Ha, ha! He is one of the Legion Lost;
   He was never meant to win.
He's a rolling stone, and it's bred in the bone;
   He's a man who won't fit in.

The Trail of 'Ninety-Eight

Gold! We leapt from our benches.
Gold! We sprang from our stools.
Gold! We wheeled in the furrow,
  fired with the faith of fools.
Fearless, unfound, unfitted,
  far from the night and the cold.
Heard we the clarion summons,
  followed the master-lure—Gold

◆

Men from the sands of the Sunland;
  men from the woods of the West;
Men from the farms and the cities,
  into the Northland we pressed.
Graybeards and striplings and women,
  good men and bad men and bold,
Leaving our homes and our loved ones,
  crying exultantly, "Gold!"

◆

Never was seen such an army,
  pitiful, futile, unfit;
Never was seen such a spirit,
  manifold courage and grit.
Never has been such a cohort
  under one banner unrolled
As surged to the ragged-edged Arctic,
  urged by the arch-tempter—Gold.

◆

"Farewell!" we cried to our dearests;
little we cared for their tears.
"Farewell!" we cried to the humdrum
and the yoke of the hireling years;
Just like a pack of school-boys,
and the big crowd cheered us good-bye.
Never were hearts so uplifted,
never were hopes so high.

The spectral shores flitted past us,
and every whirl of the screw
Hurled us nearer to fortune,
and ever we planned what we'd do—
Do with the gold when we got it—
big, shiny nuggets like plums,
There in the sand of the river,
gouging it out with our thumbs.

And one man wanted a castle,
another a racing stud;
A third would cruise in a palace yacht
like a red-necked prince of blood.
And so we dreamed and we vaunted,
millionaires to a man,
Leaping to wealth in our visions
long ere the trail began.

II.

We landed in wind-swept Skagway.
We joined the weltering mass,
Clamoring over their outfits,
waiting to climb the Pass.
We tightened our girths and our pack-straps;
we linked on the Human Chain,
Struggling up to the summit,
where every step was a pain.

Gone was the joy of our faces,
grim and haggard and pale;
The heedless mirth of the shipboard
was changed to the care of the trail.
We flung ourselves in the struggle,
packing our grub in relays,
Step by step to the summit
in the bale of the winter days.

◆

Floundering deep in the sump-holes,
stumbling out again;
Crying with cold and weakness,
crazy with fear and pain.
Then from the depths of our travail,
ere our spirits were broke,
Grim, tenacious and savage,
the lust of the trail awoke.

◆

For grub meant gold to our thinking,
and all that could walk must pack;
The sheep for the shambles stumbled,

each with a load on its back;
And even the swine were burdened,
and grunted and squealed and rolled,
And men went mad in the moment,
huskily clamoring, "Gold!"

"Klondike or bust!" rang the slogan;
every man for his own.
Oh, how we flogged the horses,
staggering skin and bone!
Oh, how we cursed their weakness,
anguish they could not tell,
Breaking their hearts in our passion,
lashing them on till they fell!

Oh, we were brutes and devils,
goaded by lust and fear!
Our eyes were strained to the summit;
the weakling dropped to the rear,
Falling in heaps by the trail-side,
heart-broken, limp, and wan;
But the gaps closed up in an instant,
and heedless the chain went on.

Never will I forget it,
there on the mountain face,
Antlike, men with their burdens,
clinging in icy space;

Dogged, determined and dauntless,
cruel and callous and cold,
Cursing, blaspheming, reviling,
and ever that battle-cry—"Gold!"

◆

Thus toiled we, the army of fortune,
in hunger and hope and despair,
Till glacier, mountain and forest
vanished, and, radiantly fair,
There at our feet lay Lake Bennett,
and down to its welcome we ran:
The trail of the land was over,
the trail of the water began.

◆

III.

We built our boats and we launched them.
Never has been such a fleet;
A packing-case for a bottom,
a mackinaw for a sheet.
Shapeless, grotesque, lopsided,
flimsy, makeshift and crude,
Each man after his fashion
builded as best be could.

Each man worked like a demon,
as prow to rudder we raced;
The winds of the Wild cried "Hurry!"
the voice of the waters, "Haste!"
We hated those driving before us;
we dreaded those pressing behind;
We cursed the slow current that bore us;
we prayed to the God of the wind.

Spring! and the hillsides flourished,
vivid in jewelled green;
Spring! and our hearts; blood nourished
envy and hatred and spleen.
Little cared we for the Spring-birth;
much cared we to get on—
Stake in the Great White Channel,
stake ere the best be gone.

The greed of the gold possessed us;
  pity and love were forgot;
Covetous visions obsessed us;
  brother with brother fought.
Partner with partner wrangled,
  each one claiming his due;
Wrangled and halved their outfits,
  sawing their boats in two.

Thuswise we voyaged Lake Bennett,
  Tagish, then Windy Arm,
Sinister, savage and baleful,
  boding us hate and harm.
Many a scow was shattered
  there on that iron shore;
Many a heart was broken
  straining at sweep and oar.

We roused Lake Marsh with a chorus,
  we drifted many a mile.
There was canyon before us—
  cave-like its dark defile;
The shores swept faster and faster;
  the river narrowed to wrath;
Waters that hissed disaster
  reared upright in our path.

Beneath us the green tumult churning,
above us the cavernous gloom;
Around us, swift twisting and turning,
the black, sullen walls of a tomb.
We spun like a chip in a mill-race;
our hearts hammered under the test;
Then—oh, the relief on each chill face!—
we soared into sunlight and rest.

Hand sought for hand on the instant.
Cried we, "Our troubles are o'er!"
Then, like a rumble of thunder,
heard we a canorous roar.
Leaping and boiling and seething,
saw we a cauldron afume;
There was the rage of the rapids,
there was the menace of doom.

The river springs like a racer,
sweeps through a gash in the rock;
Butts at the boulder-ribbed bottom,
staggers and rears at the shock;
Leaps like a terrified monster,
writhes in its fury and pain;
Then with the crash of a demon
springs to the onset again.

79

Dared we that ravening terror;
  heard we its din in our ears;
Called on the Gods of our fathers,
  juggled forlorn with our fears;
Sank to our waists in its fury,
  tossed to the sky like a fleece;
Then, when our dread was the greatest,
  crashed into safety and peace.

But what of the others that followed,
  losing their boats by the score?
Well could we see them and hear them,
  strung down that desolate shore.
What of the poor souls that perished?
  Little of them shall be said—
On to the Golden Valley!
  Pause not to bury the dead.

Then there were days of drifting,
  breezes soft as a sigh;
Night trailed her robe of jewels
  over the floor of the sky.
The moonlit stream was a python,
  silver, sinuous, vast,
That writhed on a shroud of velvet—
  well, it was done at last.

There were the tents of Dawson,
there the scar of the slide;
Swiftly we poled o'er the shallows,
swiftly leapt o'er the side.
Fires fringed the mouth of Bonanza;
sunset gilded the dome;
The test of the trail was over—
thank God, thank God, we were Home!

The Shooting of Dan McGrew

A bunch of the boys were whooping it up
in the Malamute saloon;
The kid that handles the music-box
was hitting a jag-time tune;
Back of the bar, in a solo game,
sat Dangerous Dan McGrew,
And watching his luck was his light-o'-love,
the lady that's known as Lou.

◆

When out of the night, which was fifty below,
and into the din and the glare,
There stumbled a miner fresh from the creeks,
dog-dirty, and loaded for bear.
He looked like a man with a foot in the grave

and scarcely the strength of a louse,
Yet he tilted a poke of dust on the bar,
and he called for drinks for the house.
There was none could place the stranger's face,
though we searched ourselves for a clue;
But we drank his health, and the last to drink
was Dangerous Dan McGrew.

There's men that somehow just grip your eyes,
and hold them hard like a spell;
And such was he, and he looked to me
like a man who had lived in hell;
With a face most hair, and the dreary stare
of a dog whose day is done,
As he watered the green stuff in his glass,
and the drops fell one by one.
Then I got to figgering who he was,
and wondering what he'd do,
And I turned my head—and there watching him
was the lady that's known as Lou.

His eyes went rubbering round the room,
and he seemed in a kind of daze,
Till at last that old piano fell
in the way of his wandering gaze.
The ragtime kid was having a drink;
there was no one else on the stool,

So the stranger stumbles across the room,
and flops down there like a fool.
In a buckskin shirt that was glazed with dirt
he sat, and I saw him sway;
Then he clutched the keys with his talon hands
—my God, but that man could play!

◆

Were you ever out in the Great Alone,
when the moon was awful clear,
And the icy mountains hemmed you in
with a silence you most could *hear;*
With only the howl of a timber wolf,
and you camped there in the cold,
A half-dead thing in a stark, dead world,
clean mad for the muck called gold;
While high overhead, green, yellow and red,
the North Lights swept in bars?—
Then you've a hunch what the music meant...
hunger and night and the stars.

◆

And hunger not of the belly kind
that's banished with bacon and beans,
But the gnawing hunger of lonely men
for a home and all that it means;
For a fireside far from the cares that are,
four walls and a roof above;
But oh! so cramful of cozy joy,

and crowned with a woman's love—
A woman dearer than all the world,
and true as Heaven is true...
(God! how ghastly she looks through her rouge—
the lady that's known as Lou.)

◆

Then on a sudden the music changed,
so soft that you scarce could hear;
But you felt that your life had been looted clean
of all that it once held dear;
That someone had stolen the woman you loved;
that her love was a devil's lie;
That your guts were gone, and the best for you
was to crawl away and die.
'Twas the crowning cry of a heart's despair,
and it thrilled you through and through—
"I guess I'll make it a spread misere,"
said Dangerous Dan McGrew.

◆

The music almost died away...
then it burst like a pent-up flood;
And it seemed to say, "Repay, repay,"
and my eyes were blind with blood.
The thought came back of an ancient wrong,
and it stung like a frozen lash,
And the lust awoke to kill, to kill...
then the music stopped with a crash,

And the stranger turned, and his eyes they burned
in a most peculiar way;
◆

In a buckskin shirt that was glazed with dirt
he sat, and I saw him sway;
Then his lips went in a kind of grin,
and he spoke, and his voice was calm,
And "Boys," said he, "you don't know me,
and none of you care a damn;
But I want to state, and my words are straight,
and I'll bet my poke they're true,
That one of you is a hound of hell...
and that one is Dan McGrew."
◆

Then I ducked my head and the lights went out,
and two guns blazed in the dark,
And a woman screamed, and the lights went up,
and two men lay stiff and stark.
Pitched on his head, and pumped full of lead,
was Dangerous Dan McGrew,
While the man from the creeks lay clutched to the breast
of the lady that's known as Lou.
◆

These are the simple facts of the case,
　　and I guess I ought to know.
They say that the stranger was crazed with "hooch,"
　　and I'm not denying it's so.
I'm not so wise as the lawyer guys,
　　but strictly between us two—
The woman that kissed him—and pinched his poke—
　　was the lady that's known as Lou.

The Ballad of Gum-Boot Ben

He was an old prospector with a vision bleared and dim.
He asked me for a grubstake, and the same I gave to him.
He hinted of a hidden trove, and when I made so bold
To question his veracity, this is the tale he told:

◆

"I do not seek the copper streak,
nor yet the yellow dust;
I am not fain for sake of gain
to irk the frozen crust;
Let fellows gross find gilded dross,
far other is my mark;
Oh, gentle youth, this is the truth—
I go to seek the Ark.

◆

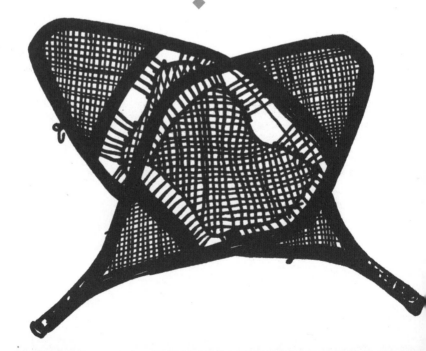

"I prospected the Pelly bed,
I prospected the White;
The Nordenscold for love of gold
I piked from morn till night;
Afar and near for many a year
I led the wild stampede,
Until I guessed that all my quest
was vanity and greed.

◆

"Then came I to a land I knew
no man had ever seen,
A haggard land, forlornly spanned
by mountains lank and lean;
The nitchies said 'twas full of dread,
of smoke and fiery breath,
And no man dare put foot in there
for fear of pain and death.

◆

"But I was made all unafraid,
so, careless and alone,
Day after day I made my way
into that land unknown;
Night after night by camp-fire light
I crouched in lonely thought;
Oh, gentle youth, this is the truth—
I knew not what I sought.

◆

"I rose at dawn; I wandered on.
'Tis somewhat fine and grand
To be alone and hold your own
in God's vast awesome land;
Come woe or weal, 'tis fine to feel
a hundred miles between
The trails you dare and pathways where
the feet of men have been.

"And so it fell on me a spell
of wander-lust was cast.
The land was still and strange and chill,
and cavernous and vast;
And sad and dead, and dull as lead,
the valleys sought the snows;
And far and wide on every side
the ashen peaks arose.

"The moon was like a silent spike
that pierced the sky right through;
The small stars popped and winked and hopped
in vastitudes of blue;
And unto me for company
came creatures of the shade,
And formed in rings and whispered things
that made me half afraid.

"And strange though be, 'twas borne on me
that land had lived of old,
And men had crept and slain and slept
where now they toil for gold;
Through jungles dim the mammoth grim
had sought the oozy fen,
And on his track, all bent of back,
had crawled the hairy men.

◆

"And furthermore, strange deeds of yore
in this dead place were done.
They haunted me, as wild and free
I roamed from sun to sun;
Until I came where sudden flame
uplit a terraced height,
A regnant peak that seemed to seek
the coronal of night.

◆

"I scaled the peak; my heart was weak,
yet on and on I pressed.
Skyward I strained until I gained
its dazzling silver crest;
And there I found, with all around
a world supine and stark,
Swept clean of snow, a flat plateau,
and on it lay—the Ark.

◆

"Yes, there, I knew, by two and two
the beasts did disembark,
And so in haste I ran and traced
in letters on the the Ark
My human name—Ben Smith's the same.
And now I want to float
A syndicate to haul and freight
to town that noble boat."

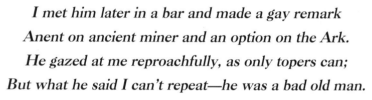

I met him later in a bar and made a gay remark
Anent on ancient miner and an option on the Ark.
He gazed at me reproachfully, as only topers can;
But what he said I can't repeat—he was a bad old man.

The Low-Down White

This is the pay-day up at the mines,
when the bearded brutes come down
There's money to burn in the streets to-night,
so I've sent my klooch to town,
With a haggard face and a ribband of red
entwined in her hair of brown.

◆

And I know at the dawn she'll come reeling home
with the bottles, one, two, three—
One for herself, to drown her shame,
and two big bottles for me,
To make me forget the thing I am
and the man I used to be.

◆

To make me forget the brand of the dog,
as I crouch in this hideous place;
To make me forget once I kindled the light
of love in a lady's face,
Where even the squalid Siwash now
holds me a black disgrace.

◆

Oh, I have guarded my secret well!
And who would dream as I speak
In a tribal tongue like a rogue unhung,
'mid the ranchhouse filth and reek,
I could roll to bed with a Latin phrase
and rise with a verse of Greek?

Yet I was a senior prizeman once,
 and the pride of a college eight;
Called to the bar—my friends were true!
 but they could not keep me straight;
Then came the divorce, and I went abroad
 and "died" on the River Plate.

◆

But I'm not dead yet; though with half a lung,
 there isn't time to spare,
And I hope that the year will see me out,
 and, thank God, no one will care—
Save maybe the little slim Siwash girl
 with the rose of shame in her hair.

◆

She will come with the dawn, and the dawn is near;
 I can see its evil glow,
Like a corpse-light seen through a frosty pane
 in a night of want and woe;
And yonder she comes by bleak bull-pines,
 swift staggering through the snow.

97

The Man from Eldorado

He's the man from Eldorado,
and he's just arrived in town,
In moccasins and oily buckskin shirt.
He's gaunt as any Indian, and pretty nigh as brown;
He's greasy, and he smells of sweat and dirt.
He sports a crop of whiskers that would shame a healthy hog;
Hard work has racked his joints and stooped his back;
He slops along the sidewalk followed by his yellow dog,
But he's got a bunch of gold-dust in his sack.

◆

He seems a little wistful as he blinks at all the lights,
And maybe he is thinking of his claim
And the dark and dwarfish cabin
where he lay and dreamed at nights,
(Thank God, he'll never see the place again!)
Where he lived on tinned tomatoes,
beef embalmed and sourdough bread,
On rusty beans and bacon furred with mold;
His stomach's out of kilter and his system full of lead,
But it's over, and his poke is full of gold.

◆

He has panted at the windlass, he has loaded in the drift,
He has pounded at the face of oozy clay;
He has taxed himself to sickness,
dark and damp and double shift,
He has labored like a demon night and day.
And now, praise God, it's over, and he seems to breathe again

Of new-mown hay, the warm, wet friendly loam;
He sees a snowy orchard in a green and dimpling plain,
And a little vine-clad cottage and it's—Home.

◆

II.

He's the man from Eldorado,
and he's had a bite and sup,
And he's met in with a drouthy friend or two;
He's cached away his gold-dust, but he's sort of bucking
up, So he's kept enough tonight to see him through.
His eye is bright and genial, his tongue no longer lags;
His heart is brimming o'er with joy and mirth;
He may be far from savory, he may be clad in rags,
But to-night he feels as if he owns the earth.

◆

Says he, "Boys, here is where the shaggy
North and I will shake;
I thought I'd never manage to get free.
I kept on making misses; but at last I've got my stake;
There's no more thawing frozen muck for me.
I am going to God's Country, where I'll live the simple life;
I'll buy a bit of land and make a start;
I'll carve a little homestead, and I'll win a little wife,
And raise ten little kids to cheer my heart."

◆

They signified their sympathy by crowding to the bar;
They bellied up three deep and drank his health.
He shed a radiant smile around and smoked a rank cigar;

They wished him honor, happiness, and wealth.

They drank unto his wife to be— that unsuspecting maid;

They drank unto his children half a score;

And when they got through drinking, very tenderly they laid

The man from Eldorado on the floor.

◆

III.

He's the man from Eldorado,

and he's only starting in

To cultivate a thousand-dollar jag.

His poke is full of gold-dust and his heart is full of sin,

And he's dancing with a girl called Muckluck Mag.

She's as light as any fairy; she's as pretty as a peach;

She's mistress of the witchcraft to beguile;

There's sunshine in her manner, there is music in her speech,

And there's concentrated honey in her smile.

◆

Oh, the fever of the dance-hall and the glitter and the shine,

The beauty, and the jewels, and the whirl,

The madness of the music, the rapture of the wine,

The languorous allurement of a girl!

She is like a lost madonna; he is gaunt, unkempt and grim;

But she fondles him and gazes in his eyes;

Her kisses seek his heavy lips, and soon it seems to him

He has staked a little claim in Paradise.

◆

"Who's for a juicy two-step?" cries the master of the floor;

The music throbs with soft, seductive beat.

There's glitter, gild and gladness; there are pretty girls galore;
   There's a woolly man with moccasins on feet.
They know they've got him going; he is buying wine for all;
   They crowd around as buzzards at a feast,
Then when his poke is empty, they boost him from the hall,
   And spurn him in the gutter like a beast.

◆

He's the man from Eldorado,
   and he's painting red the town;
   Behind he leaves a trail of yellow dust;
In a whirl of senseless riot he is ramping up and down;
   There's nothing checks his madness and his lust.
And soon the word is passed around—it travels like a flame;
   They fight to clutch his hand and call him friend,
The chevaliers of lost repute, the dames of sorry fame;
   Then comes the grim awakening—the end.

IV.

He's the man from Eldorado,
and he gives a grand affair;
There's feasting, dancing, wine without restraint.
The smooth Beau Brummels of the bar, the faro men, are there;
The tinhorns and purveyors of red paint;
The sleek and painted women, their predacious eyes aglow—
Sure Klondike City never saw the like;
Then Muckluck Meg proposed the toast: "The giver of the show,
The livest sport that ever hit the pike."

◆

The "live one" rises to his feet; he stammers to reply—
And then there comes before his muddled brain
A vision of green vastitudes beneath an April sky,
And clover pastures drenched with silver rain.
He knows that it can never be, that he is down and out;
Life leers at him with foul and fetid breath;
And then amid the revelry, the song and cheer and shout,
He suddenly grows grim and cold as death.

◆

He grips the table tensely, and he says, "Dear friends of mine,
I've let you dip your fingers in my purse;
I've crammed you at my table,
and I've drowned you in my wine,
And I've little left to give you but—my curse.
I've failed supremely in my plans; it's rather late to whine;
My poke is mighty weasened up and small.

I thank you each for coming here; the happiness is mine—
And now, you thieves and harlots, take it all."

◆

V.

He twists the thong from off his poke; he swings it o'er his head;
The nuggets fall around their feet like grain.
They rattle over roof and wall; they scatter, roll and spread;
The dust is like a shower of golden rain.
The guests a moment stand aghast, then grovel on the floor;
They fight, and snarl, and claw, like beasts of prey;
And then, as everybody gabbed and everybody swore,
The man from Eldorado slipped away.

◆

He's the man from Eldorado,
and they found him stiff and dead,
Half covered by the freezing ooze and dirt.
A clotted Colt was in his hand, a hole was in his head,
And he wore an old and oily buckskin shirt.
His eyes were fixed and horrible, as one who hails the end;
The frost had set him rigid as a lot;
And there, half lying on his breast, his last and only friend,
There crouched and whined a mangy yellow dog.

The Harpy

There was a woman, and she was wise; woefully wise was she;
She was old, so old, yet her years all told were but a score and three;
And she knew by heart, from finish to start, the Book of Iniquity.

There is no hope for such as I
on earth, nor yet in Heaven;
Unloved I love, unloved I die,
unpitied, unforgiven;
A loathed jade, I ply my trade,
unhallowed and unshriven.

I paint my cheeks, for they are white,
and cheeks of chalk men hate;
Mine eyes with wine I make to shine,
that man may seek and sate;
With overhead a lamp of red
I sit me down and wait

◆

Until they come, the nightly scum,
with drunken eyes aflame;
Your sweethearts, sons, ye scornful ones—
'tis I who know their shame.
The gods, ye see, are brutes to me—
and so I play my game.

◆

For life is not the thing we thought,
and not the thing we plan;
And Woman in a bitter world
must do the best she can—
Must yield the stroke, and bear the yoke,
and serve the will of man;

◆

Must serve his need and ever feed
the flame of his desire,
Though be she loved for love alone,
or be she loved for hire;
For every man since life began
is tainted with the mire.

◆

And though you know he love you so
and set you on love's throne;
Yet let your eyes but mock his sighs,
and let your heart be stone,
Lest you be left (as I was left)
attainted and alone.

◆

From love's close kiss to hell's abyss
is one sheer flight, I trow,
And wedding ring and bridal bell
are will-o'-wisps of woe,
And 'tis not wise to love too well,
and this all women know.

◆

Wherefore, the wolf-pack having gorged
upon the lamb, their prey,
With siren smile and serpent guile
I make the wolf-pack pay—
With velvet paws and flensing claws,
a tigress roused to slay.

One who in youth sought truest truth
and found a devil's lies;
A symbol of the sin of man,
a human sacrifice.
Yet shall I blame on man the shame?
Could it be otherwise?

Was I not born to walk in scorn
where others walk in pride?
The Maker marred, and, evil-starred,
I drift upon his tide;
And He alone shall judge His own,
so I His judgment bide.

Fate has written a tragedy; its name is "The Human Heart."
The Theatre is the House of Life, Woman the mummer's part;
The Devil enters the prompter's box, and the play is ready to start.

The Ballad of One-Eyed Mike

This is the tale that was told to me
by the man with the crystal eye,
As I smoked my pipe in the campfire light,
and the Glories swept the sky;
As the Northlights gleamed and curved and streamed,
and the bottle of "hooch" was dry.

A man once aimed that my life be shamed,
and wrought me a deathly wrong;
I vowed one day I would well repay,
but the heft of his hate was strong.
He thonged me East and he thonged me West;
he harried me back and forth,
Till I fled in fright from his peerless spite
to the bleak, bald-headed North.

And there I lay, and for many a day
I hatched plan after plan,
For a golden haul of the wherewithal
to crush and to kill my man;
And there I strove, and there I clove
through the drift of icy streams;
And there I fought, and there I sought
for the pay-streak of my dreams.

So twenty years, with their hopes and fears
and smiles and tears and such,
Went by and left me long bereft
of hope of the Midas touch;
About as fat as a chancel rat,
and lo! despite my will,
In the weary fight I had clean lost sight
of the man I sought to kill.

◆

'Twas so far away, that evil day
when I prayed to the Prince of Gloom
For the savage strength and the sullen length
of life to work his doom.
Nor sign nor word had I seen or heard,
and it happed so long ago;
My youth was gone and my memory wan,
and I willed it even so.

◆

It fell one night in the waning light
by the Yukon's oily flow,
I smoked and sat as I marvelled at
the sky's port-winey glow;
Till it paled away to an absinthe gray,
and the river seemed to shrink,
All wobbly flakes and wriggling snakes
and goblin eyes a-wink.

◆

'Twas weird to see and it 'wildered me
in a queer hypnotic dream,
Till I saw a spot like an inky blot
come floating down the stream;
It bobbed and swung; it sheered and hung;
it romped round in a ring;
It seemed to play in a tricksome way;
it sure was a merry thing.

◆

In freakish flights strange oily lights
came fluttering round its head,
Like butterflies of a monster size—
then I knew it for the Dead.
Its face was rubbed and slicked and scrubbed
as smooth as a shaven pate;
In the silver snakes that the water makes
it gleamed like a dinner-plate.

◆

It gurgled near, and clear and clear
and large and large it grew;
It stood upright in a ring of light
and it looked me through and through.
It weltered round with a woozy sound,
and ere I could retreat,
With the witless roll of a sodden soul
it wantoned to my feet.

◆

And here I swear by this Cross I wear,
I heard that "floater" say:
"I am the man from whom you ran,
the man you sought to slay,
That you may note and gaze and gloat,
and say 'Revenge is sweet,'
In the grit and grime of the river's slime
I am rotting at your feet.

"The ill we rue we must e'en undo,
though it rive us bone from bone;
So it came about that I sought you out,
for I prayed I might atone.
I did you wrong, and for long and long
I sought where you might live;
And now you're found, though I'm dead and drowned,
I beg you to forgive."

So sad it seemed, and its cheek-bones gleamed,
and its fingers flicked the shore;
And it lapped and lay in a weary way,
and its hands met to implore;
That I gently said: "Poor, restless dead,
I would never work you woe;
Though the wrong you rue you can ne'er undo,
I forgave you long ago."

Then, wonder-wise, I rubbed my eyes
and I woke from a horrid dream.
The moon rode high in the naked sky,
and something bobbed in the stream.
It held my sight in a patch of light,
and then it sheered from the shore;
It dipped and sank by a hollow bank,
and I never saw it more.

◆

This was the tale he told to me,
that man so warped and gray,
Ere he slept and dreamed, and the camp-fire gleamed
in his eye in a wolfish way—
That crystal eye that raked the sky
in the weird Auroral ray.

The Law of the Yukon

This is the law of the Yukon,

and ever she makes it plain:

"Send not your foolish and feeble;

send me your strong and your sane—

Strong for the red rage of battle;

sane, for I harry them sore;

Send me men girt for the combat,

men who are grit to the core;

Swift as the panther in triumph,

fierce as the bear in defeat,

Sired of a bulldog parent,

steeled in the furnace heat.

◆

"Send me the best of your breeding,

lend me your chosen ones;

Them will I take to my bosom,

them will I call my sons;

Them will I gild with my treasure,

them will I glut with my meat;

But the others—the misfits, the failures—

I trample them under my feet.

Dissolute, damned and despairful,

crippled and palsied and slain,

Ye would send me the spawn of your gutters—

Go! take back your spawn again!

◆

"Wild and wide are my borders,
stern as death is my sway;
From my ruthless throne I have ruled alone
for a million years and a day;
Hugging my mighty treasure,
waiting for man to come,
Till he swept like a turbid torrent,
and after him swept—the scum.
The pallid pimp of the dead-line,
the enervate of the pen,
One by one I weeded them out,
for all that I sought was—Men.

◆

"One by one I dismayed them,
frighting them sore with my glooms;
One by one I betrayed them
unto my manifold dooms.
Drowned them like rats on my rivers,
starved them like curs on my plains,
Rotted the flesh that was left them,
poisoned the blood in their veins;
Burst with my winter upon them,
searing forever their sight,
Lashed them with fungus-white faces,
whimpering wild in the night;

◆

"Staggering blind through the storm-whirl,
stumbling mad through the snow,

Frozen stiff in the ice-pack,
brittle and bent like a bow;
Featureless, formless, forsaken,
scented by wolves in their flight,
Left for the wind to make music,
through ribs that are glittering white;
Gnawing the black crust of failure,
searching the pit of despair,
Crooking the toe in the trigger,
trying to patter a prayer;

"Going outside with an escort,
raving with lips all afoam,
Writing a check for a million,
driveling feebly of home;
Lost like a louse in the burning...
or else in the tented town
Seeking a drunkard's solace,
sinking and sinking down;
Steeped in the slime at the bottom,
dead to a decent world,
Lost 'mid the human flotsam,
far on the fontier hurled;

"In the camp at the bend of the river,
with its dozen saloons aglare,
Its gambling dens ariot,
its gramophones all ablare;

Crimped with the crimes of a city,
sin-ridden and bridled with lies,
In the hush of my mountained vastness,
in the flush of my midnight skies.
Plague-spots, yet tools of my purpose,
so natheless I suffer them thrive,
Crushing my Weak in their clutches,
that only my Strong may survive.

◆

"But the others, the men of my mettle,
the men who would 'stablish my fame
Unto its ultimate issue,
winning me honor, not shame;
Searching my uttermost valleys,
fighting each step as they go.
Shooting the wrath of my rapids,
scaling my ramparts of snow;
Ripping the guts of my mountains,
looting the beds of my creeks,
Them will I take to my bosom,
and speak as a mother speaks.

◆

"I am the land that listens,
I am the land that broods;
Steeped in eternal beauty,
crystalline waters and woods.
Long have I waited lonely,
shunned as a thing accurst,

Monstrous, moody pathetic,
the last of the lands and the first;
Visioning campfires at twilight,
sad with a longing forlorn,
Feeling my womb o'er-pregnant
with the seeds of cities unborn.

◆

"Wild and wide are my borders,
stern as death is my sway,
And I wait for the men who will win me—
and I will not be won in a day;
And I will not be won by weaklings,
subtle, suave and mild,
But by men with the hearts of Vikings,
and the simple faith of a child;
Desperate, strong and resistless,
unthrottled by fear or defeat,
Them will I gild with my treasure,
Them will I glut with my meat.

◆

"Loftly I stand from each sister land,
patient and wearily wise,
With the weight of a world of sadness
in my quiet, passionless eyes;
Dreaming alone of a people,
dreaming alone of a day,
When men shall not rape my riches,
and curse me and go away;

Making a bawd of my bounty,
fouling the hand that gave—
Till I rise in my wrath and I sweep on their path
and I stamp them into a grave;

◆

"Dreaming of men who will bless me,
of women esteeming me good,
Of children born in my borders
of radiant motherhood,
Of cities leaping to stature,
of fame like a flag unfurled,
As I pour the tide of my riches
in the eager lap of the world."

◆

This is the law of the Yukon,
that only the Strong shall thrive;
That surely the Weak shall perish,
and only the Fit survive.
Dissolute, damned and despairful,
crippled and palsied and slain,
This is the Will of the Yukon—
Lo, how she makes it plain!